LET's TALK EMOTIONS

Helping Children with Social Cognitive Deficits, Including AS, HFA, and NVLD, Learn to Understand and Express Empathy and Emotions

Teresa A. Cardon
M.A., CCC-SLP

APC

Autism Asperger Publishing Co.
P.O. Box 23173
Shawnee Mission, KS 66283-0173
www.asperger.net

© 2004 Autism Asperger Publishing Co.
P.O. Box 23173
Shawnee Mission, KS 66283-0173
www.asperger.net

**Publisher's Cataloging-in-Publication
(Provided by Quality Books, Inc.)**

Cardon, Teresa A.
     Let's talk emotions : helping children with social
cognitive disorders, including AS, HFA, and NVLD, learn
to understand and express empathy and emotions / Teresa
A. Cardon
     p. cm.
     Includes bibliographical references.
     Library of Congress Control Number: 2004106925
     ISBN 1-931282-59-5

     1. Autistic children--Rehabilitation. 2. Asperger's
syndrome--Patients--Rehabilitation. 3. Nonverbal
learning disabilities. I. Title.

RC553.A88C37 2004   618.92'858803
                          QBI33-2043

This book is designed in Salsa and Tekton.

Managing Editor: Kirsten McBride
Editorial Assistance: Ginny Biddulph

Printed in the United States of America

*Dedicated to Craig, Rylee & Breelyn,
who inspire me every day!*

TABLE OF CONTENTS

INTRODUCTION

Social cognitive deficits are one of the major characteristics of Asperger Syndrome, high-functioning autism and nonverbal learning disabilities. Individuals with social cognitive deficits (SCD) struggle to participate in and maintain conversations, interact with peers, follow rules such as turn-taking, respond to social cues, including body language, and, in general, have difficulty relating in a natural, effective way with others.

Social cognitive deficits can be particularly debilitating because they are not outwardly apparent. That is, children with SCD typically look no different than their peers, so when they behave in apparently contradictory and sometimes bizarre ways, they may offend or upset a communication partner, thereby damaging the relationship. Compounding these difficulties is the fact that many persons with SCD are not aware that the relationship has been damaged and, therefore, make no attempt to repair it by apologizing or otherwise explaining or changing their behavior (Attwood, 1998). Also, they do not understand why their attempts to communicate and interact with others are often unsuccessful.

Since these challenges are neurologically based, children with SCD do not pick up cues from their environment as do other children as part of their natural development. Consequently, they need direct, specific instruction to learn the subtle nuances required in successfully interpreting social situations.

Group sessions to facilitate social interactions are becoming an integral element of intervention programs for children with SCD, and social skills training has become a major focus of many psychologists, speech pathologists, teachers and other professionals. A number of social skills programs are now commercially available. In particular, the work of Michelle Garcia Winner has been effective in increasing the social success of children with SCD (Winner, 2000). Her strategies are designed specifically to teach children about perspective taking by encouraging them to "think about you thinking about me." Her books provide explicit group session activities and ideas for teaching social thinking to children with SCD.

Another helpful resource is Jed Baker's *Social Skills Training for Children and Adolescents with Asperger Syndrome and Social-Communication Problems* (Baker, 2003). The book focuses on what skills to target as well as instructional strategies, behavior management techniques and ways to encourage generalization of learned social skills. Another aid in guiding social interactions among children with SCD is Pamela Wolfberg's *Peer Play and the Autism Spectrum: The Art of Guiding Children's Socialization and Imagination* (Wolfberg, 2003), which introduces the Integrated Play Groups model. This model supports children who are "novice players," those with autism spectrum disorders, in interactions with "expert players," that is, typical peers and siblings, through mutually enjoyed play experiences.

Despite progress in recent years in terms of social skills training of children with SCD, one area that has been greatly overlooked is that of emotions. Children with SCD have difficulty identifying emotions, not only in other people, but in themselves as well. The abstract features involved in deciphering others' reactions and emotions, including facial expressions, body language, tone and voice inflection, present significant problems. Thus, these children have difficulty following or even detecting nonverbal cues, leaving them at an incredible disadvantage when considering that over 90% of all communication is nonverbal. For example, if a child has difficulty recognizing sarcasm in others, she may be unable to understand that she has upset a friend or teacher responding "thanks a lot" in a given situation in a sarcastic tone of voice accompanied by an exasperated roll of the eyes. Indeed, the child with SCD most likely will think that the "thanks" is sincere, totally missing the hidden message (Myles, Trautman, & Schelvan, 2004).

Similarly, parents express frustration because their child with SCD does not "see" when they are angry. A parent may become upset because the child has created a huge mess in the recently cleaned family room or turned his nose up at a specially prepared meal. The child's inaccurate interpretations of others' behavior in these situations are often viewed as rude due to a failure to apologize, comply with requests, and so on. But, in fact, such reactions are totally lost on the child.

Children with SCD are also at an increased risk for establishing false friendships because they do not recognize when they are being taken advantage of. This is particularly disturbing as many of these children so desperately want to make friends. In an era of increased bullying at school and in the community, children with SCD are "perfect targets" (Heinrichs, 2003).

Again, due to their difficulty in interpreting others' words and actions, children with SCD are often said to lack empathy; that is, they are unaware of how another person feels. That does not mean that they are unable to care about another person (Attwood, 1998), however. There is an important distinction here. The ability to care about another person is called "sympathetic empathy," whereas the ability to relate to and recognize another's feelings is considered "intellectual empathy" (Guttman, 2000). With respect to children with SCD, it is "intellectual empathy" parents and others are referring to, whether they realize it or not, when they state that their child lacks empathy (Kennedy, 2002). In truth, children with SCD not only lack the ability to recognize the feelings of another person, they lack "intellectual empathy" toward their own feelings as well. For example, when a child is angry and is asked why she is upset, she may respond, "I don't know," or come up with an explanation that is totally unrelated to the situation that appears to have set off the anger. In other words, the child is truly unaware of her emotional triggers.

The apparently nonchalant attitude of many children with SCD tends to exacerbate things even further. Thus, they are often viewed as outwardly defiant and disrespectful when, in reality, they simply missed or misinterpreted certain of the nonverbal cues in the environment. During group projects, for example, lack of perspective taking combined with the inability to interpret others' emotions is manifested when a child goes on and on about an area of special interest even if others show signs of boredom or total lack of interest. In such situations, peers often do not take time to explain how they feel, but merely move on, thereby excluding the child with SCD from friendships or social interactions. Unaware of these dynamics, the child becomes frustrated and may lash out, claiming that the other kids are being unfair. Sometimes such frustration escalates, causing the child to lose control emotionally, what Kari Dunn Buron (2003) calls their "autism gets too big."

Children with SCD also lack the specific vocabulary necessary to express the types of emotions they are experiencing, which can cause further misunderstanding and extreme frustration. Thus, many children with SCD are limited to a few terms, which they use over and over to describe emotional scenes. For example, if shown pictures depicting sad, angry and hurt and asked what emotions they represent, a child may respond with the term "depressed." That is, while able to recognize that the pictures may all be similarly grouped, the child is unable to verbalize the subtle differences in each picture. The lack of specific vocabulary contributes to the "intellectual empathy" difficulties mentioned earlier.

Another area of concern is that children with SCD often display their emotions in ways that are considered inappropriate, as in the group setting above. Parents and teachers describe children as going from 0 to 10 on an "emotions thermometer" in a matter of seconds, with 0 being calm and 10 being furious, sometimes for no obvious reason. What makes this particularly problematic for others is that, in some instances, the child is reacting to a frustrating event that occurred earlier and is just now manifesting itself. Indeed, the child himself may not be fully aware of the reason behind his emotional outburst. Quite often peers are unsure of how to respond to a child who is "overreacting" like that. As a result, they stay away, perpetuating the isolation and limited peer interaction the child already faces. Buron and Curtis (2003) show how something as simple as a 5-point scale can help children understand their own emotional responses to daily events that might otherwise cause an emotional overreaction.

Indeed, such overreaction has been identified as one of the causes behind the teasing that is frequently directed at children with SCD (Heinrichs, 2003). Thus, the child's overly "dramatic" style sometimes gratifies and encourages a bully. On the reverse side, some children with SCD are viewed as bullies themselves. At times, they may intentionally provoke anger and hurt, or otherwise encourage negative feelings in a peer to study the emotional response displayed. For example, a child may recreate the negative reaction that occurred in response to hitting a child at the lunch table by hitting another child later on. In other instances, a child with SCD becomes aggressive, physically or verbally, as a last resort – when no other option seems available to deal with a frustrating episode.

The difficulty many individuals with SCD have in making and maintaining friends is partly due to the fact that they do not feel comfortable and are often unaware of how to share personal information about themselves. While typically developing children relatively easily find commonalities between themselves and others to create a bond of friendship, children with SCD tend to focus on surface information. If you ask these children to tell you about their friends, for example, they often discuss their outward appearance instead of something qualitative such as being fun or kind, being a good friend, and so on.

THE PURPOSE OF THIS BOOK

As teachers, parents and clinicians, we must work to break down the abstract concepts that are involved with "intellectual empathy" and teach children with SCD in the most concrete and cognitive manner possible. We must break down feelings and emotions piece by piece and smile by smile.

The purpose of *Let's Talk Emotions* is to guide parents, teachers and others in doing just that. The following collection of activities may be used with children of various ages and levels of cognitive ability, but the final goal is always the same: To teach children with SCD to identify and respond to their own feelings as well as the feelings of others, thereby improving their existing social relationships and increasing their chances of success in future social endeavors.

HOW TO USE THIS BOOK

The book is intended for use with small groups of children with the assistance of a facilitator. Speech pathologists, psychologists, special and general educators, and parents and family members are all encouraged to use the book as a tool to guide children with SCD. The activities require varying degrees of emotional awareness for children to be successful. Start with the more concrete activities, like providing definitions or identifying specific parts of the face involved with facial expressions, and then move into more abstract areas such as role-plays. The activities can be adjusted for difficulty and age level in many different ways as pointed out throughout.

A great tool to use in conjunction with the suggested activities is the concept of Social Stories™. A Social Story "describes a situation, concept, or social skill using a format that is meaningful for people with ..." (Gray, 2002, pp. 13-1) social cognitive deficits.

A Social Story consists of three main parts: descriptive sentences, directive sentences and perspective sentences. A *descriptive sentence* describes the situation, concept or social skill that is being addressed. The *directive sentence* provides instructions or direction on how to approach or handle the situation, concept or social skill being addressed. Finally, the *perspective sentence* gives insight into the internal state of mind of the participants. Several Social Stories are included in the Appendix as examples (e.g., p. A1). However, Social Stories are particularly beneficial when written to address the specific needs of the individual involved, so practice with the format and come up with some great ones on your own to suit the particular child with whom you are working.

For ease of use, each activity is presented on a separate page organized in a consistent format around the following headings: goal, age range, materials, activity and notes. The "notes" section is intended to help you keep track of progress and to note when an adjustment in the activity has been made that works better for a particular child; for example, activities may be combined by taking parts of one and using them in another. Be creative and remember – emotions are not an exact science.

Finally, be sure that discussions accompany every activity. Whenever appropriate, prompt students to reflect on their behavior by asking such questions as: Why is it important to think about how someone else feels? Why do I want someone else to know how I feel? Do other people feel similar things? What can I gain from looking at pictures of facial expressions? How does role-playing an emotion help in the real world? These are new and often confusing concepts we are asking children to think about, so it is important that we talk them through each smile and frown every step of the way.

GoАLs АNd ObjECTivEs

A list of possible goals and objectives are introduced on pages 9-12. The goals are broken down into two categories: "external focus" and "internal focus." Goals that are listed under "external focus" are meant to assist the child in recognizing the emotional states of another person, whereas goals listed under "internal focus" are intended to aid the child in identifying and dealing with his or her own emotions. The goal objectives listed refer to specific lesson plans and activities found throughout the book. For example, the goal on page 11 that states "Student will use an emotions thermometer to depict what he is feeling" refers to activities on pages 15 & 16.

In turn, the activities all refer back to an "external focus" or "internal focus" goal to provide a direct link between the intervention that is being provided and the goals that are being addressed. The emotions thermometer worksheet activity on page 16, for example, refers to the "internal focus" goal on page 11, which states "To help strengthen personal identification and expression of feelings." Again, this directly links the activities to the target goals, ensuring a clear and concise plan of action.

When determining goal mastery, keep in mind that emotions are not an exact science. Mastery will need to focus on each specific emotion. For example, a child may have mastered "sad" and "happy" on an emotions thermometer and still not yet understand "angry." Be aware that mastery of one emotion during an activity does not mean mastery of all emotions during the activity. Remember, we must teach emotions frown by frown and smile by smile.

I have been fortunate to work with many children and grown-ups alike who helped to train me as a therapist in the most effective ways of treating and teaching individuals with social cognitive deficits. It is because of their help that I have had great success using the activities presented here in working with children with social cognitive deficits. I am excited to share my experiences with you.

— Teresa A. Cardon

GoALs & ObJEcTivEs: ExTERNAL Focus (OTHERs)

To help strengthen "intellectual empathy":

1. Student will identify emotions by providing the appropriate name when shown a picture stimulus in 7 out of 10 trials.

   a. When given an emotion picture card, the student will verbalize the depicted emotion from a list of the possible answers.

   b. When given an emotion picture card, the student will verbalize the depicted emotion.

   c. When looking through a magazine, the student will identify the target emotion.

2. Student will determine which factors help in identifying a target emotion in 7 out of 10 trials.

   a. The student will define facial expression, tone, body language and voice inflection.

b.   When shown a specific emotion (sad, happy, depressed, angry, etc.), the student will provide different attributes, facial expressions, tone, body language and voice inflection, that may accompany the target emotion.

c.   While looking at the facilitator or some other group member's emotional portrayal, the student will identify the four facial attributes being presented.

3. **Student will identify a target emotion during role-play in 7 out of 10 trials.**

a.   When the facilitator portrays an emotion, the student will identify the target emotion.

b.   When group members portray an emotion, the student will identify the target emotion.

4. **Student will determine how different events elicit various emotions and the cause-and-effect relationships between each event and the corresponding emotions in 7 out of 10 trials.**

a.   The student will create a story and determine the emotional response of the characters during differing events.

b.   The student will identify the different emotions that can be experienced during a particular incident.

c.   While discussing sporting events, the student will identify what emotions are present when various outcomes occur during the game (losing/winning).

GoAls & ObJEcTivEs: INTERNAL Focus (SELF)

To help strengthen personal identification and expression of feelings:

1. **Student will use an emotions thermometer to depict what he is feeling in 7 out of 10 trials.**

   a. The student will define emotions using dictionaries as well as his own definitions of the target emotion.

   b. The student will identify situations in which she has felt the target emotion.

   c. The student will depict what he is feeling using the emotions thermometer during structured class time activities such as circle time, speech therapy, group work, and so on.

2. **Student will keep an emotions journal to identify feelings and emotions that occur throughout the week for 9 out of 10 weeks.**

   a. The student will write about one daily event during which she experienced an identifiable emotion.

b. The student will write about an event where she was unable to label a specific emotion.

c. The student will write freely about emotional experiences.

3. **Student will practice various expressions of emotions in 7 out of 10 trials.**

   a. The student will use a mirror to practice facial expressions of target emotions.

   b. The student will use different types of body language to express the target emotion.

   c. The student will practice different tones of voice to depict the target emotion.

   d. The student will utilize varying degrees of vocal inflection to depict a target emotion.

4. **Student will identify appropriate vs. inappropriate ways in which to respond to various emotional states in 8 out of 10 trials.**

   a. When given a picture stimulus, the student will provide three appropriate and three inappropriate responses.

   b. When given a hypothetical situation, the student will identify three appropriate and three inappropriate responses.

   c. When role-playing with group members, the student will identify three appropriate and three inappropriate responses.

ACTIVITIES

Emotions Thermometer

Goal
To help strengthen personal identification and expression of feelings

Age Range
4 years-18 years

Materials
- Emotions thermometer, one for each student (A2-A6)
- Social Story (A1)
- Markers

Activity
An emotions thermometer plays an integral role in emotion training. Children can help create their own thermometer with the worksheets in the Appendix. For younger children, include four to six emotions: sad, angry, hurt, happy, surprised, scared. For older children, use the emotions thermometer provided or fill in the emotions on a blank thermometer.

When children enter the room, they can use the thermometer to indicate how they are feeling. That is, as they sit down at the table, children can move the arrow on the thermometer to express how they are feeling at the time. Be sure to probe and ask if they would like to discuss their feelings further. It may be helpful to establish a routine "check-in" period at the beginning of group time. Be sure to set clear time lines for how long check-in will last because children with SCD may get upset if you try to end their speaking turn before they feel they have finished. Using a timer of some sort to establish a set limit clearly indicates the rules and expectations ahead of time and makes transitions easier.

After children are comfortable using the emotions thermometer, give them a copy to keep at home. Be sure to speak with the child's parents about the check-in process that encourages feelings to be discussed. A Social Story is included in the Appendix (A1) that will help the child, family members and caregivers better understand how to use the emotions thermometer. Children are often able to use the thermometer to identify emotions much sooner than they are able to discuss them, so further discussion may be some time away. It all depends on the individual child.

Notes:

EMOTIONS THERMOMETER WORKSHEETS

GOAL
To help strengthen personal identification and expression of feelings

AGE RANGE
8 years-18 years

MATERIALS
- Emotions thermometer worksheets (A7-A17), one for each student
- Pens, pencils

ACTIVITY
To increase success using the emotions thermometer, discussing definitions, perspective taking and problem solving is imperative. The worksheets may be used during group time or sent home for homework. Regardless of how they are used, be sure that each emotion is discussed. It is very important that a child has a definition that she can understand in order for the emotions thermometer to hold personal meaning. Therefore, both a dictionary and a personal meaning are included. The perspective-taking piece allows children to identify when they or others may have felt the target emotion.

NOTES:

EMOTIONS DICTIONARY

GOAL
To help strengthen personal identification and expression of feelings

AGE RANGE
8 years-18 years

MATERIALS
- Definition worksheet (A33), one for each student
- Pens, pencils
- Dictionary

ACTIVITY
Before children can successfully identify facial features, they must first know what exactly is meant by "facial features." Use the definition worksheet in the Appendix (A33) to encourage discussion of the following features: facial expression, tone, body language, and voice inflection.

NOTES:

PicTuRE JouRNaL

GoAl
To help strengthen personal identification and expression of feelings

AgE RaNgE
5 years-18 years

MaTERiALs
- Picture journal worksheets (A21-A32), one for each student
- Markers

AcTiviTY
To help younger children identify their own feelings and emotions, a picture journal is very helpful. Help the children verbalize "I feel _____ when . . ." and then encourage them to draw a picture to match the statement. The child may not have the vocabulary to precisely express how she is feeling, but drawing a picture often helps. You can use the emotions on an emotions thermometer if they are appropriate, or come up with your own.

OldER ChildREN
Older children also enjoy the picture journal activity. They can use the lines to write a couple of brief sentences, but the main expression is done through the picture they draw. Drawing has been very successful even for older children, particularly when they have difficulty finding the "right" words to use when trying to write about their feelings. They often feel more comfortable sharing a picture journal than a written one, and it can lead to some important discussions. For example, I have seen children draw pictures of events that they were unable to describe clearly with words. Too often, using words to discuss events that were very frustrating leaves the child with SCD feeling misunderstood. Through pictures the actual happenings of the event may become more apparent, and a discussion of the details drawn on the paper can then take place.

NoTEs:

EmoTioNs JouRNal

GoAl
To help strengthen personal identification and expression of feelings

AgE RaNgE
8 years-18 years

MATERiALs
- Composition book or other appropriate space for journaling, one for each student
- My Emotions Journal (A20), one for each child
- Pens, pencils

AcTiviTY
To help children identify their own feelings and emotions, it is imperative that they keep an emotions journal. Encourage them to write in it on a daily basis. They can write before they go to bed as a type of check-in or they can use it as a tool when they are frustrated. For example, if a child comes home from school and appears to be agitated, encourage him to write about it in his journal. Similarly, if the child seems annoyed about something that happened at church, again, encourage her to use a journal.

Journaling is often less threatening than trying to verbally describe one's frustration. I have been told by many parents how helpful it has been in de-escalating their child's problem. Children may not have the necessary vocabulary to precisely express how they are feeling, but the journal provides a forum for expression to begin. It is an outlet for the emotional experiences that can be overwhelming. Instead of getting worked up again by trying to talk about the event, the children can find a quiet place to be by themselves and write. That act alone can help in decreasing their frustration.

Be sure to establish the private nature of the journal ahead of time. If children would like to share information from their journal, they may do so, but they should not be pressured to do it. I often glue the "directions" for the journal on the inside cover (A20).

NoTEs:

EMOTIONS DETECTIVE

GOAL
To help strengthen "intellectual empathy"

AGE RANGE
5 years-13 years

MATERIALS

- Magnifying glass, one per child
  (you can make them out of cardstock or use actual magnifying glasses)
- Detective worksheet (A35), one for each child
- Emotion picture cards (any cards that depict facial emotions will do – school supply stores or therapy catalogs have several different varieties; also see References under COLORCARDS)
- Story Organizer worksheet (A34), one for each child

ACTIVITY

In this activity, children become "emotions detectives." There are several ways to conduct this activity. First, if space allows, hang emotions picture cards around the room and identify the target emotion. The children then use their magnifying glass to identify the emotion. Whoever finds the emotion first and is correct, gets to pick the next emotion. In a slight variation, you can write out different emotions on pieces of paper, put them in a hat or other container and randomly choose the target emotion.

Another variation is to pick the Emotion of the Week and provide the children with an emotions worksheet that encourages them to be on the look-out for the specified emotion all week. They can identify the emotion in themselves as well as in others. During class the following week, the children can share what their detective work uncovered and then put the "evidence" in their work folder.

Be sure to introduce a Social Story (see page 6) before children set out to find their target emotions. They have to be instructed on how to appropriately identify the emotion to ensure that an embarrassing situation does not develop. For example, if they spot someone crying, encourage them not to yell out with excitement at having found the target emotion and risk causing an embarrassing moment.

OLDER CHILDREN
The older children can use the Story Organizer worksheet (A34) to identify the rising and falling action surrounding the situations where they notice that the emotion is present.

NOTES:

MAGAZINE CUT-OUTS

GOAL
To help strengthen "intellectual empathy"

AGE RANGE
5 years-13 years

MATERIALS
- Magazines that appeal to children
- Scissors
- Glue
- Cardstock, a sheet per child
- Popsicle sticks (6-8 per child)

ACTIVITY
Using pictures of real people is a great way to create awareness of the numerous ways in which the human face can express emotion. With younger children, introduce one emotion at a time. It is good to start with the basics – happy, sad, tired, angry – as these are usually the easiest for children to recognize. Go through the pages of a magazine until the child recognizes a picture depicting the particular emotion. Depending on the child's level, more or less support in finding the pictures may be necessary. For example, children 8 and under often need specific guidance in recognizing emotions. Help the children stop and really look at each picture they find. Children over the age of 8 can work more independently, but remember that children with SCD have trouble with facial expressions in general so be sure to offer suggestions. This is not a test, we want them to be as successful as possible in finding each emotion.

Once a picture has been found, help the child cut out the face and glue it onto a piece of cardstock, attach a popsicle stick to the base and create an emotion puppet. It is helpful to write the emotion on the back of the "emotion puppet" to ensure consistency in the wording across all the participants throughout the child's day. The children can take their puppets with them and play guessing games with mom and dad, teachers or others. The children will benefit from continued exposure to the faces and the emotion terms.

OLDER CHILDREN

Older children can identify magazine pictures of the target emotion themselves and then cut them out and glue all the pictures of one emotion onto a piece of cardstock. When the assignment is completed, the student will have a picture book with pages of various emotions: happy, sad, tired, angry, confused, frustrated, bored, etc. If a child would like to look for more than one emotion at a time and can handle the quick shifts in thought, set up several pages at once. Parents can get involved in the process as well. If a child runs into a picture that he thinks would fit, parents should encourage him to either cut it out or make a copy of it to add to the book.

NOTES:

Flannel Faces

Goal
To help strengthen "intellectual empathy"

Age Range
4 years-11 years

Materials
 Flannel board

 Cut-outs in the shape of a face, ears, nose, eyes, eyebrows and several different mouths (you may use felt pieces or copy pages A52-A54. Color and laminate them and place a piece of Velcro on the back).

Activity
It is fun to just play with the different faces and discover the various expressions that can be made. In the process, the child becomes aware of how every part of the face can be used to express emotions. This hands-on activity aids the child in acquiring a more concrete way to recognize different emotions.

For younger children, it is helpful to talk about each piece individually and assist the children in placing the pieces on the flannel board or other surface. Once the basic pieces of the face are in place, change one piece at a time to talk about the target emotion. For example, to talk about sad, turn the smile upside down and verbalize the action of "making a frown." Then angle the eyebrows to depict a sad face and verbalize that the "eyebrows frown, too." Finally, let the children practice making the faces sad. Do not introduce too many emotions at once. Stick with the basics: sad, angry, happy, tired, surprised.

Older Children
When working with older children, allow them to create the first face and then help them determine which facial features have to be rearranged in order to create the target emotion. The students can take turns creating their own faces and then have the other children try to guess what the target emotion is. Be sure to point out which features change to indicate the target emotion. Older children also enjoy making silly faces with the flannel pieces. Follow their lead and see what emotion terms they can come up with to describe the faces they create.

Notes:

MiRRoR, MiRRoR . . .

GoAl

To help strengthen "intellectual empathy"

AgE RANgE

5 years-12 years

MATERIAls

- Emotion picture cards (commercial or teacher-made)
- Large mirror or small hand-held mirrors

AcTiviTY

Place emotion picture cards face down on the table. Have the children choose a card. Ask them to look in a mirror and depict the emotion portrayed on the card they have chosen. Other group members try to guess what emotion the child is trying to portray.

The kids have a lot of fun making faces at themselves. They have to focus carefully on each individual part of the face. Are my eyebrows raised or lowered? Do I need to open or lower my eyelids? Is my mouth open or closed? Do I show teeth? All these small nuances are the things we want them to be aware of.

NoTEs:

"Today I Feel Silly"

Goal

To help strengthen personal identification and expression of feelings

Age Range

4 years-12 years

Materials

 Book – *Today I Feel Silly* by Jamie Lee Curtis (see References)

Activity

Reading books about emotions and feelings is another helpful tool. One book that we often use to start out a session is *Today I Feel Silly*. The group facilitator, a parent or professional, can read the book to the children and lead a conversation about the emotions presented.

This book discusses the different types of moods that children experience every day. It also points out that whatever mood a child is experiencing is okay, and therefore validates his or her feelings. Finally, it allows children to talk about how they are feeling, including how they are feeling about coming to social skills training.

I have found it useful to keep an eye out for children's books that describe or discuss emotions. I have a library of books that we read together, and I also let families borrow the books to encourage conversations about emotions at home.

Notes:

IF YOU'RE HAPPY, SAD, MAD ...

GOAL
To help strengthen personal identification and expression of feelings

AGE RANGE
3 years-7 years

MATERIALS
 Large mirror, if possible; smaller individual mirrors will do

ACTIVITY
With young children, singing songs is a great way to talk about emotions. A classic is "If You're Happy and You Know It ..." You can add to this song to include a variety of emotions.

If you're happy and you know it, clap your hands (CLAP, CLAP)
If you're happy and you know it, clap your hands (CLAP, CLAP)
If you're happy and you know it, then your face will surely show it (POINT TO FACE)
If you're happy and you know it clap your hands (CLAP, CLAP)

If you're sad and you know it, you can cry BOO-HOO (RUB EYES AND PRETEND TO CRY)
(repeat following above format)

If you're mad and you know it, you can shout "I'm Mad!" (BANG FISTS ONTO LEGS)
(repeat following above format)

If you're sleepy and you know it, go to sleep (HANDS UP AS PILLOW, EYES SHUT)
(repeat following above format)

Children love to watch themselves and others in the mirror to see all the faces they can create. The mirrors provide great feedback of their facial expressions. Singing this song as an opening activity as well as a closing activity brings consistency to the session.

NOTES:

EMOTIONS SCAVENGER HUNT

GOAL

To help strengthen personal identification and expression of feelings

AGE RANGE

5 years–13 years

MATERIALS

- Emotion picture cards (commercial or teacher-made)
- Written lists of emotions, one per child (alter the way in which each list is ordered; for example, List 1 – happy, sad, angry. List 2 – sad, angry, happy, and so on)

ACTIVITY

Hide or tape various emotion cards around the room and have the children go on a scavenger hunt to find them. Provide the children with an emotions list. The children now have to find the emotions on their list in the correct order. (This is why it is helpful to alter the order of emotions on each list – each child goes to different pictures instead of them all going to the same picture at the same time.) Once all the children have identified their list of emotions, gather the picture cards and go through the pile one by one to see if the children were able to correctly match the emotions term with the corresponding picture card.

This is a great activity to do when children are first being introduced to emotion therapy. The children don't feel a lot of pressure to get the correct answer. Each child searches individually, and then a group discussion of specific facial cues can further their understanding. The difficulty of the terms and pictures can be increased as students' skill level increases.

NOTES:

Koosh Ball Toss

Goal

To help strengthen "intellectual empathy"

Age Range

5 years-9 years

Materials

- ☺ Emotion picture cards (commercial or teacher-made)
- ☺ Koosh balls or bean bags

Activity

Koosh Ball Toss is a great activity for younger children. You can play the game in a couple of slightly different ways.

1. Turn the emotion cards face down on the carpet and have the children take turns throwing a koosh ball onto the cards. The closest card to the koosh ball is the one the child picks up and tries to identify. You may provide them with prompts in the beginning and then try to build up to independent identification. By providing prompts in the beginning, you can ensure some success and decrease the level of frustration. This activity is great when you are first introducing emotion therapy. Be sure to start out with pictures that are very different from each other, happy, sad, tired, and angry, to ensure as much success as possible. Increase the difficulty with a greater number of cards with more similar pictures: angry, sad, upset, etc.

2. For a slightly different twist, lay the cards face up and call out an emotion. The child then attempts to throw the koosh ball onto the corresponding picture card. Again, be sure to start out simple with few cards. Also, make sure that children have a chance to point to the card they were aiming for if the koosh ball is difficult for them to manage.

Notes:

CREATE-A-STORY

GOAL
To help strengthen "intellectual empathy"

AGE RANGE
8 years-18 years

MATERIALS
- Emotion picture cards (commercial or teacher-made)
- Story Organizer worksheet (A34)

ACTIVITY
Choose an emotion picture card and ask the child to create the story that is presented in the picture. Using the Story Organizer worksheet, help the child identify rising and falling actions around the events depicted. For example, if the picture depicts two people arguing, the child can determine what led up to the argument, what the argument was about, the relationship between those arguing, as well as some ways to end the argument. The activity can be completed orally or in writing.

Being able to develop a narrative story is an important element of perspective taking, which is usually difficult for children with social cognitive deficits. The activity requires the children to think about others in order to create different characters in their story, forcing them to put themselves in someone else's shoes, so to speak. They must create events and determine emotional outcomes to these events while taking into account how all of the characters feel about the same event. This requires a great deal of "thinking about others" (Winner, 2002) — a task that does not come easy to a child with SCD. Guide the activity to ensure success and gradually back off as the child becomes familiar with the task and with what is expected.

NOTES:

PHOTO SHOOT

GOAL

To help strengthen "intellectual empathy"

AGE RANGE

8 years-18 years

MATERIALS

- Disposable camera(s)
- Written list of emotions, one for each (you may use the hand-drawn pictures in the Appendix, A55-A65, to provide more visual cues to younger groups)
- Mirror

ACTIVITY

Have a disposable camera handy when those perfect faces appear! When a child displays some great facial features or body language that is right-on, snap a picture and create a scrapbook for the group to refer to and enjoy. You can also ask the children to pose for each emotion, but be sure to verbally describe the features involved (facial expressions and body language) with the emotion and examine the emotion pictures with students before you begin. They can also practice in a mirror. The feedback children get from seeing themselves portraying emotions is priceless.

Another variation of Photo Shoot is to give each child a disposable camera of their own. The children then have a great opportunity to catch family members and friends experiencing and portraying various emotions (real or acted out). Through this process the children can also create picture cards for practice at home. Provide the children with a list of emotions and encourage them to become photographers for the week!

NOTES:

Emotions Charades

Goal
To help strengthen "intellectual empathy"

Age Range
8 years-18 years

Materials
- Emotion picture cards (commercial or teacher-made)
- Koosh ball

Activity
Place several picture cards upside down on the floor and have the children take turns throwing the koosh ball onto one of the cards. The child picks up the card that the koosh ball landed on or is closest to. It is the child's responsibility to act out the emotion depicted on the card. Be aware of children's level and stage, and prompt with ideas as needed. The other children take turns guessing which emotion is being depicted. The child who guesses correctly must describe the various things, facial expressions, body language, voice inflection, and tone, that led him to the correct conclusion. The child who guesses correctly takes a turn throwing the koosh ball, and the game continues.

This game should be introduced only after the four identifying features (facial expressions, body language, voice inflection, and tone) have been discussed in some detail and are fairly well understood by the children.

Notes:

EMOTIONS BINGO

GOAL
To help strengthen "intellectual empathy"

AGE RANGE
8 years-18 years

MATERIALS
- Bingo cards (A39-A43); photocopy a card for each student
- Markers/chips
- Picture cards

ACTIVITY
There are a couple of different ways to play Emotions Bingo.

1. To start the game, call out an emotion. In order to place a chip on that emotion, the children must act it out first. The students can work together and create a small skit (this works well with older children), or they can simply express the emotion from their own perspective.

2. To spice things up a bit, act out the emotion before calling it out. The children then take turns identifying the emotion. If they identify the emotion correctly (working together with group members may be helpful), they may place a chip on their bingo card. When a child covers a row of emotions, she wins the game.

NOTES:

POSTER BOARD ART

GOAL
To strengthen "intellectual empathy"

AGE RANGE
5 years-12 years

MATERIALS
- Poster board
- Scissors
- Tape
- Faces coloring worksheets (A55-A65), one of each sheet per child
- Markers

ACTIVITY
Take several large pieces of poster board and label each with a title emotion: Happy, Sad, Angry, etc. Hand out photo copies of the Faces coloring worksheets. Each child colors and then cuts out his or her own pictures. It is the child's responsibility to place the picture on the appropriate poster board. The finished products are great to hang up around the room for reference.

An alternative is to use Velcro on the poster board and the backs of the faces so that the activity may be done over and over. It is also fun to mix up the faces and have the children take them down and put them in the right place. This requires careful scrutiny and strengthens their ability to identify facial features.

NOTES:

CREATE-A-POSTER

GOAL
To strengthen "intellectual empathy"

AGE RANGE
8 years-18 years

MATERIALS
- Poster board, one sheet per child
- Magazines
- Markers
- Glue
- Dictionary
- Glitter
- Yarn
- Buttons
- Scissors

Create-a-Poster is a fun activity that allows children to express themselves creatively. Assign each child a different emotion, or let them pick one, and hand out poster board. The children can clip out magazine pictures, draw a scene, list the characteristics of the emotion, tell a story – the possibilities are endless. Then let them get as creative as they would like with buttons, yarn, foam pieces, glitter, etc., to personalize the poster. Some children may need more guidance than others, but for the most part this is their activity, so let them create at will.

Hang up the posters around the room for a while. The unique aspects of each poster, even those showing the same emotion, will do more to educate children than we can imagine.

NOTES:

CAREER EMOTIONS

GOAL
To strengthen "intellectual empathy"

AGE RANGE
8 years-18 years

MATERIALS
- Pictures of different careers
- Books about different careers
- Paper, pens

ACTIVITY
What types of emotions are associated with different careers? Have the children talk about what they would like to be when they grow up. Find books with pictures depicting different jobs and include them in your discussion. Teacher supply stores usually have great resources. Suggest different careers to help get the discussion going. Talk about emotions connected with various jobs: childcare worker, mother, CEO, bus driver, teacher, grocery clerk, computer technician, airplane pilot, fire fighter, doctor, etc. For example, discuss the joy a childcare worker feels when she is hugged and the frustration she might feel if a child hits or bites. Similarly, a pilot may feel elated when he flies a plane, but nervous and possibly scared if things go wrong.

Take this activity one step further and have the children interview a person in their chosen career field. Guide the group in coming up with a list of questions to ask. For example, what things about your job make you feel happy? Are there things about your job that are frustrating? Why do you like your job? Do people get angry with you at work? Have the children choose 7-10 questions that they like and have them write them down on a piece of paper.

Practice interviewing each other during group time. The children will need a step-by-step guide of how to set up the interview: 1. Call and schedule an appointment (in person or over the phone). 2. Have your list of questions with you during the interview. 3. Bring a tape recorder (get permission ahead of time) or write down the person's responses. 4. Be sure to thank the person for the interview.

This activity will put students' conversational skills and knowledge of emotions to the test!

NOTES:

MOVIE CRITICS

GOAL

To strengthen "intellectual empathy"

AGE RANGE

8 years-18 years

MATERIALS

- List of role-plays (A37-A38) cut into strips
- Hat, bowl or other container

ACTIVITY

Cut the list of role-plays into individual strips and place them in a container. Choose your role-play at random and have the children act as movie critics. Act alone or with another child to perform skits together. Possible ideas include: You lose five dollars, how do you feel? You find five dollars, how do you feel? A visit to the doctor or dentist, how do you feel? Your pet frog died, how do you feel? You got an "A" on a paper, how do you feel? The goal of the rest of the group members is to respond by identifying the target emotion and "critique" the performance. For example, "I really felt your pain when your frog died." Or "Thumbs up on your excitement at finding five dollars!"

As the children get more comfortable with the activity, let two children take over the acting responsibilities while you join in with the movie critics.

NOTES:

WHEEL OF EMOTIONS

GOAL
To strengthen "intellectual empathy"

AGE RANGE
8 years-18 years

MATERIALS
- Butcher paper
- Markers
- Crayons
- Wheel of Emotions worksheet (A36), one for each student

ACTIVITY
Create a wheel of emotions on a large piece of butcher paper. Write one emotion at the top. Now, going clockwise, have the children think of what the original emotion can lead to. Be sure to create scenarios that will help them identify the next step. Try to get them all the way around the wheel, from the original emotion and back to it again, using different emotions and scenarios. Use a different emotion at the top of the wheel to get a different outcome. For ideas, see the examples in the Appendix (A36).

This activity is very important because it reinforces the idea that emotions can facilitate both positive and negative events.

NOTES:

GREETING CARDS

GOAL
To strengthen "intellectual empathy"

AGE RANGE
8 years-18 years

MATERIALS
- Cardstock, at least one piece per child
- Markers
- Crayons
- Assortment of sample greeting cards

ACTIVITY
If you have ever purchased a greeting card, you know how many possibilities there are and how difficult it can be to find the right one. In this activity, the children create their own greeting card, but buy a few to serve as samples for the group. Be sure to include get-well, sympathy, new baby, surprise, congratulations cards, and so on, so the children can see the variety there is to choose from.

First, tell them to decide on the type of card that they would like to create – get-well, love for family member or teacher, friendship, and so on. Then hand them the cardstock and markers and let them create their own. Be sure to leave the examples out for their review – only to get ideas, not to copy. Emphasize that they must create original faces, poems, pictures, sayings, and so on. Also, the cards must include both pictures and words so that the children experience putting words to the pictured emotions. Encourage them to create more than one card each.

This activity usually works best once the children have had some exposure to emotion therapy. At that point, they have more vocabulary and have seen numerous picture cards.

NOTES:

SocK PuPPETs

GoAl
To help strengthen "intellectual empathy"

AgE RANgE
4 years-11 years

MATERiAls
- Socks
- Foam pieces
- Buttons
- Yarn
- Tacky glue
- Scissors
- Flannel faces (A52-A54)
- Large cardboard box
- Material for curtains

AcTiviTY
Create your own sock puppets to represent different emotions. Put your hand in the sock and demonstrate how the puppets work. Then place a mark where the eyes, nose and mouth have to be glued in order for the puppets to function properly. The children can make eyes out of buttons and hair out of yarn. They can also use foam pieces (can be found at any craft store) for eyebrows and a mouth to help create the appropriate emotion. It may be helpful to have the pieces pre-cut and then let the children do the gluing depending on their skill level. Older children enjoy cutting the foam pieces themselves.

You can even create a puppet theater out of a large cardboard box. Cut a hole in one side and hang some curtains. The children enjoy decorating the theater as well. Creating scenes with their puppets is a great way to express emotions. Have the kids act out why the sad puppet is sad and help him become happy. What made the angry puppet angry? Why is the grouchy puppet so grouchy? What surprise was in store for the surprised puppet?

The puppets also come in handy when children are having difficulty expressing themselves. Many children are better able to disclose information to the puppet than to you or other adults, so be sure to keep a few sock puppets on hand.

NoTEs:

ANIMAL EMOTIONS

GOAL
To help strengthen personal identification and expression of feelings

AGE RANGE
4 years-9 years

MATERIALS
- Papers
- Crayons
- Animal pictures (magazines, coloring books, etc.)
- Scissors
- Glue
- Stapler

ACTIVITY
We associate various animals with different emotions. Have the children create an animal emotion book with laughing hyenas, sly snakes, curious monkeys, a tired sloth, bubbly baboons, growling bears, etc. They can draw pictures of the animals and then label them with an emotion. They can also use animal pictures from magazines, coloring books, zoo field trips – be creative! Once they have finished their book, the children get to act like an animal and everyone else tries to guess what they are!

NOTES:

"OuTbuRsT"

GoAl

To help strengthen "intellectual empathy"

AgE RaNgE

8 years-18 years

MaTERiALs

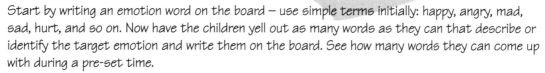

- Poster board
- Markers
- Tape

AcTiviTY

Start by writing an emotion word on the board – use simple terms initially: happy, angry, mad, sad, hurt, and so on. Now have the children yell out as many words as they can that describe or identify the target emotion and write them on the board. See how many words they can come up with during a pre-set time.

Once you have a good list, transfer the target word and the list of "outbursts" to a piece of poster board and hang it up in the room. The children can add to the list over time as they think of more words to describe the target emotion.

Knowing that the list is up in the room, the children usually go home thinking about the emotions. They will try all week long to find more words.

NoTEs:

FiNish THE STORY

GoAl
To help strengthen personal identification and expression of feelings

AgE RANgE
8 years-18 years

MATERiAls
- Paper
- Pencil
- Role-play list (A37-A38)

AcTiviTY
Choose a scenario from the role-play list and write a sentence on the board. "The boy's bird died and he felt _____ because . . ." "Your mom brought you a surprise from the mall and you felt _____ because . . .". It is helpful to include the word "because" to ensure that the children expand the story. Explain that they are going to create the rest of the story, verbally or in writing. The activity can be done as a group with each person adding one line to the story while the adult writes down the story on the board, or the children can write their own story and work independently. Be sure to address the emotional aspect of the situation.

You can change the activity slightly by asking the children to write down first a positive and then a negative way to handle the situation depicted in the role-play. Continue trying to get them to expand on the story so they can see the consequence or reward associated with a given action. For example, in the scenario where mom brings a surprise from the mall, the children could think of a negative way to handle the situation – "I'm angry at mom because I didn't get to go to the mall and pick it out myself." Or, a positive reaction – "I'm happy with mom and say thank you."

It is important to discuss acceptable and unacceptable behavior in various situations because it is not always apparent to children with SCD. They need the consequences clearly explained to them. For example, "If I am angry at mom for bringing a surprise, mom won't feel like bringing nice things home for me again." "If I say thank you for a surprise, mom will be pleased and enjoy doing special things for me." Children with SCD need scenarios broken down into very concrete steps.

NoTEs:

"EMOTION LAND"

GOAL
To strengthen "intellectual empathy"

AGE RANGE
8 years-18 years

MATERIALS
- Markers/chips
- Dice
- Photocopies of the Emotion Land game board (A44-A45) and cut-out cards (A46-A51)

ACTIVITY

The children can roll the dice to see who goes first. From then on, they roll the dice and move forward the designated number of spaces on the game board. If they land on a square that says "EMOTION," they draw an emotion card. The cards depict positive and negative situations. Depending on how they answer the question on the card, the children can move forward one space or move back one. If they provide an appropriate way to handle the situation, they get to move forward one space; if they give an inappropriate answer, they move back one space.

An alternative way to play this game is to have the children draw a card each time they roll the dice. When they land on an "EMOTION" square, they have to act out an emotion while the other group members try to guess what it is. If the group can guess what emotion the student is trying to express, she gets to move forward a space.

This game is helpful because children see "consequences" of negative behaviors and "rewards" for positive behaviors. They can also attempt to repair a negative response with a more positive one to help them learn that they are in control of their reactions. For example, if the response to the card "Someone ruined your art project that was hanging on the wall at school" is "I would punch them in the stomach," a discussion of consequences and a more appropriate solution would be warranted. The child then has a chance to move forward instead of back.

NOTES:

SPORT DAY

GOAL
To help strengthen "intellectual empathy"

AGE RANGE
8 years-18 years

MATERIALS
- Paper
- Crayons
- Markers

ACTIVITY
Sporting events often involve a wide range of emotions (sadness when the team loses, happiness when it wins, etc.). Help the children create a story involving their favorite sporting event. You can write a list of sports on the board and cover as many as you have time for to incorporate more than one favorite sport.

Ask the children to come up with the events that make up the "game." For example, if they choose baseball, they must create a story to talk about: the player who gets a hit, the player who strikes out, the great pitch that is made, the fielder who missed the ball, the fan whose team wins, and the fan whose team loses. You are the scribe who guides the writing. Eventually, an entire story about feelings involved with a game of baseball will emerge. The children can then draw pictures to go with the story. Each child can contribute one picture for a group story, or you can make copies of the story and let each child illustrate his or her own.

Almost any sporting event that the children are familiar with will do. This activity also helps children who have a hard time with organized sports because of the intense emotions involved. Guiding the perspective taking of all participants is an important tool! For example, the fielder who missed the ball is sad and frustrated, but the hitter is thrilled and excited that the fielder missed the ball. You can even elicit different emotions depending on whose "team" you are on.

NOTES:

COLOR CHART

GOAL
To help strengthen "intellectual empathy"

AGE RANGE
4 years-18 years

MATERIALS
- Paper
- Crayons
- Markers
- Book – *Don't Take It So Literally* by D. Legler (see References)

ACTIVITY
Colors are often associated with emotions (e.g., red is usually associated with anger). Create an emotions color chart to illustrate this concept. The children can draw a color spectrum of their own and then talk about the different types of feelings that people associate with each color. Explain that a color can have more than one emotion attached to it. For example, black can be associated with both anger and sadness. Red or black = angry, blue = sad, yellow = happy, green = jealous, etc.

This is a great opportunity to bring figurative language into your lesson, which causes problems for many children with SCD due to their literal interpretation of things and their limited perspective taking. For example, why do people say they are feeling "blue"? What does "red in the face" mean? How about "green with envy"? *Don't Take It So Literally* (Legler, 1991) is a useful workbook that breaks down everyday expressions piece by piece and is a great tool for this activity.

NOTES:

Light & Dark Feelings

Goal
To help strengthen "intellectual empathy"

Age Range
8 years-18 years

Materials
- Sheets of paper, one per child
- Pencils
- Emotions thermometer (A2-A6)

Activity
The terms "light" and "dark" are often associated with different emotions. Have the children fold a piece of paper in half and write "light" at the top of one half and "dark" at the top of the other. Talk about the types of feelings that might go under each category. You can use the feelings on the emotions thermometer or create a list of your own. Have the children list emotions on either side according to the discussion. It is okay if they are not all the same, but if a child puts happy on the dark side, discuss how that might not work out as well. Give children a chance to explain why they chose a particular category. For example, if surprise ends up on the dark side, maybe it signifies that the children don't like the unexpected aspects that accompany a surprise, or maybe they simply misunderstood.

Notes:

POETRY

GOAL
To help strengthen personal identification and expression of feelings

AGE RANGE
8 years-18 years

MATERIALS
- Paper
- Pencils
- Emotions thermometer (A2-A6)
- Poems – *Where the Sidewalk Ends* by S. Silverstein (see References)

ACTIVITY
For centuries, people have been describing how they feel through poetry. Read some poems to the class. Shel Silverstein's *Where the Sidewalk Ends* is a fabulous choice for children because the poems are about subjects they identify with, and they contain simple language. Children can pick an emotion to write a poem about or you can assign an emotion if they are having trouble deciding on their own. Encourage students to let their creation reign free. Be sure to let them know that their poems can remain private. They don't have to share with the group, but if they would like to, they are welcome, so save some time for a poetry reading. You will be surprised how many budding Shakespeares you may have in your group.

NOTES:

Emotions Collages

Goal
To help strengthen "intellectual empathy"

Age Range
5 years-18 years

Materials
- Poster board
- Magazines and other materials for collages
- Scissors
- Glue
- Markers
- Art supplies

Activity
Have the children create art collages expressing emotions. Choose the emotion that the group will work on. Have the children find faces in magazines, coloring books, hand drawn art, etc., that depict the target emotion. Have them glue the pieces onto a large piece of poster board. Each child may have his or her own piece of poster board or they may work as a group. They can expand the initial selection to scenes and objects if they can justify why it applies to the emotion. Let them get creative with markers and craft supplies, and you will have just created some great artwork for the room!

Notes:

REFERENCES

Attwood, T. (1998). *Asperger's Syndrome – A guide for parents and profession-als*. London: Jessica Kingsley Publishers.

Baker, J. E. (2003). *Social skills training for children and adolescents with Asperger Syndrome and social-communication problems*. Shawnee Mission, KS: Autism Asperger Publishing Company.

Baron-Cohen, S. (1995). *Mindblindness: An essay on autism and theory of mind*. Boston: The MIT Press.

COLORCARDS. (1997). *Emotion & expression cards*. www.Sourceresource.com.

Curtis, J. (2001). *Today I feel silly and other moods that make my day*. New York: Joanna Cotler Books, an Imprint of HarperCollins Publishers.

Buron, K. D. (2003). *When my autism gets too big! A relaxation book for children with autism spectrum disorders*. Shawnee Mission, KS: Autism Asperger Publishing Company.

Buron, K. D., & Curtis, M. (2003). *The incredible 5-point scale. Assisting stu-dents with autism spectrum disorders in understanding social interac-tions and controlling their emotional responses*. Shawnee Mission, KS: Autism Asperger Publishing Company.

Franke, L. (2001). *Coaching comprehension & creating conversation*. Long Beach, CA: Orange County Department of Education S.U.C.S.E.S.S. Project.

Goldstein, A., & McGinnis, E. (1997). *Skillstreaming the adolescent: Revised edi-tion*. Chicago: Research Press.

Gray, C. (2002). *The new social story book*. Ft. Worth, TX: Future Horizons.

Greenspan, S. (1998, July). *Affirming autistic culture: Inclusion isn't everthing*. Keynote Speaker at the Autism Society of America National Convention, Reno, NV.

Guttman, H. (2000, September). Empathy in families of women with borderline personality disorder, anorexia nervosa, and a control group. *Family Process*. [Electronic version]. Oxford, UK: Blackwell Publishing.

Heinrichs, R. (2003). *Perfect targets: Asperger Syndrome and bullying –
Practical solutions for surviving the social world.* Shawnee Mission, KS:
Autism Asperger Publishing Co.

Kennedy, D. (2002). *The ADHD autism connection.* Colorado Springs, CO:
Waterbook Press.

Legler, D. (1991). *Don't take it so literally.* Youngtown, AZ: ECL Publications.

Myles, B. S., & Trautman, M. L., & Shelvan, R. L. (2004). *The hidden curriculum:
Practical solutions for understanding unstated rules in social situations.*
Shawnee Mission, KS: Autism Asperger Publishing Company.

Winner, M. (2000). *Inside out: What makes a person with social cognitive deficits
tick?* San Jose, CA: Michelle Garcia Winner Publishing.

Silverstein, S. (1974). *Where the sidewalk ends.* New York: Harper Collins
Publishers.

APPENDIX

LisT oF MATERiALS

MY EmoTioNs THERmomETER
(Social Story)

This is my emotions thermometer! It will help me to learn about and talk about my feelings.

I can move the arrow up and down to help express how I feel. I will learn all about the emotions on my thermometer during my social skills group.

Other people can look at my emotions thermometer to see how I feel.

I can talk about my feelings if I want to. This will help others understand why I am feeling the way that I am.

Most of the time I will feel better when people understand my feelings. My parents and teachers will be pleased that I am learning to talk about my feelings.

Note: This Social Story may be used in combination with the emotions thermometer activity (p. 15).

A1

EMOTIONS THERMOMETER

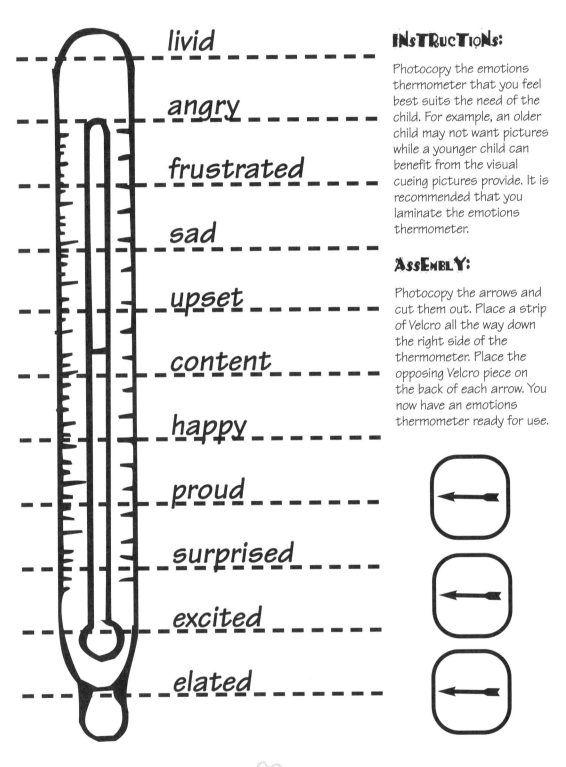

livid

angry

frustrated

sad

upset

content

happy

proud

surprised

excited

elated

INSTRUCTIONS:

Photocopy the emotions thermometer that you feel best suits the need of the child. For example, an older child may not want pictures while a younger child can benefit from the visual cueing pictures provide. It is recommended that you laminate the emotions thermometer.

ASSEMBLY:

Photocopy the arrows and cut them out. Place a strip of Velcro all the way down the right side of the thermometer. Place the opposing Velcro piece on the back of each arrow. You now have an emotions thermometer ready for use.

A2

From: *Let's Talk Emotions: Helping Children with Social Cognitive Disorders, Including AS, HFA, and NVLD, Learn to Understand and Express Empathy and Emotions* (2004) by Teresa A. Cardon. Shawnee Mission, KS: Autism Asperger Publishing Company; www.asperger.net. Copied with permission.

EMOTIONS THERMOMETER
(Young ages)

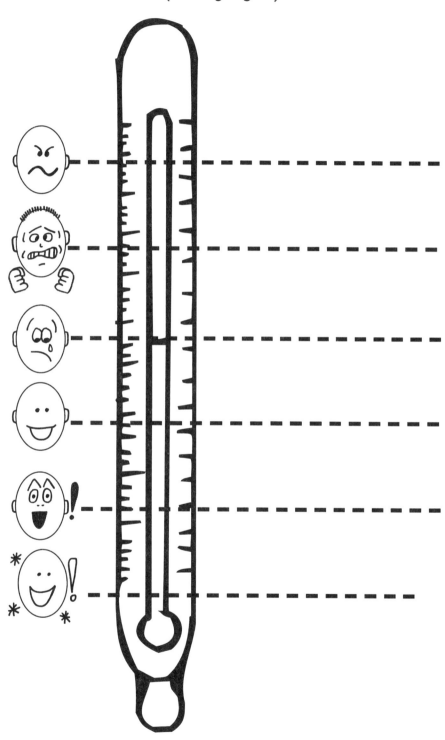

EMOTIONS THERMOMETER
(Young ages)

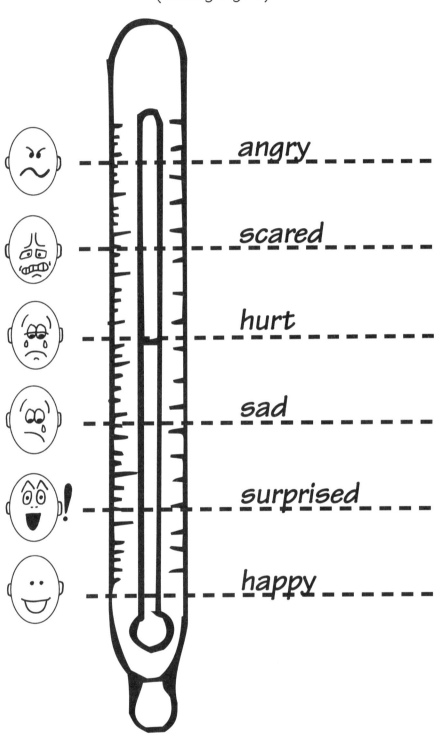

angry

scared

hurt

sad

surprised

happy

A4

EMOTIONS THERMOMETER
(Older ages)

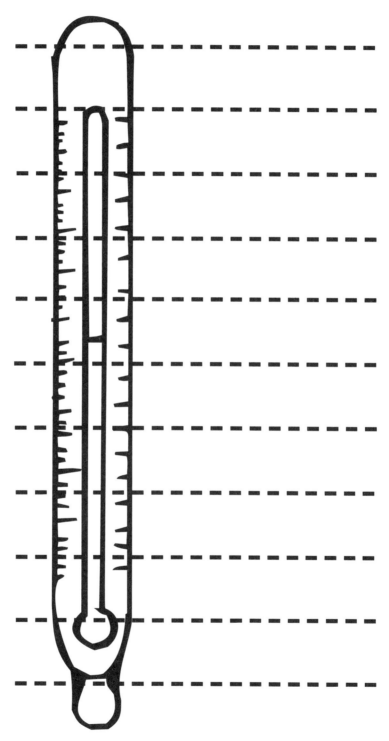

A5

EMOTIONS THERMOMETER

(Older ages)

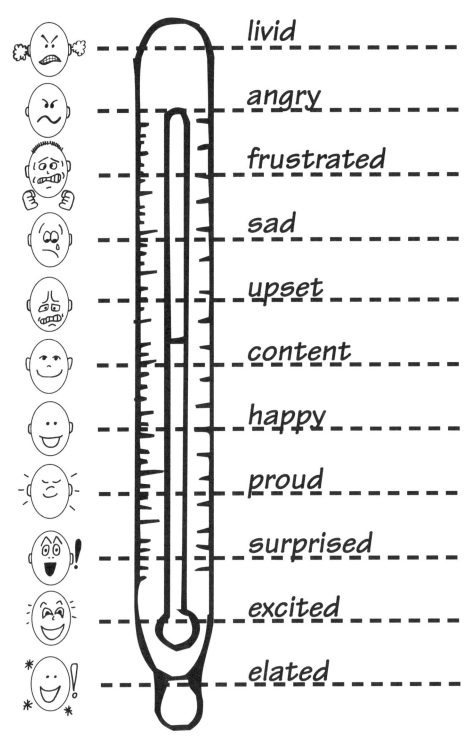

livid

angry

frustrated

sad

upset

content

happy

proud

surprised

excited

elated

A6

From: *Let's Talk Emotions: Helping Children with Social Cognitive Disorders, Including AS, HFA, and NVLD, Learn to Understand and Express Empathy and Emotions* (2004) by Teresa A. Cardon. Shawnee Mission, KS: Autism Asperger Publishing Company; www.asperger.net. Copied with permission.

Emotion: Livid

Defining

Dictionary Definition: _____

_____

_____

My Definition: _____

_____

_____

Perspective Taking

I have felt _____ when: _____

_____

_____

I noticed someone else was _____ when: _____

_____

_____

Problem Solving

When I feel _____ I can:

1. _____

2. _____

3. _____

4. _____

A7

EMOTION: ANGRY

DEFINING

Dictionary Definition: _____

_____

_____

My Definition: _____

_____

_____

PERSPECTIVE TAKING

I have felt _____ when: _____

_____

_____

I noticed someone else was _____ when: _____

_____

_____

PROBLEM SOLVING

When I feel _____ I can:

1. _____

2. _____

3. _____

4. _____

A8

EMOTION: FRUSTRATED

DEFINING

Dictionary Definition: _____

_____

_____

My Definition: _____

_____

_____

PERSPECTIVE TAKING

I have felt _____ when: _____

_____

_____

I noticed someone else was _____ when: _____

_____

_____

PROBLEM SOLVING

When I feel _____ I can:

1. _____

2. _____

3. _____

4. _____

A9

EmoTion: Sad

DeFining

Dictionary Definition: _____

_____

_____

My Definition: _____

_____

_____

PersPecTive TAKing

I have felt _____ when: _____

_____

_____

I noticed someone else was _____ when: _____

_____

_____

ProblEm Solving

When I feel _____ I can:

1. _____

2. _____

3. _____

4. _____

A10

Emotion: Upset

Defining

Dictionary Definition: _____

_____

_____

My Definition: _____

_____

_____

Perspective Taking

I have felt _____ when: _____

_____

_____

I noticed someone else was _____ when: _____

_____

_____

Problem Solving

When I feel _____ I can:

1. _____

2. _____

3. _____

4. _____

A11

From: *Let's Talk Emotions: Helping Children with Social Cognitive Disorders, Including AS, HFA, and NVLD, Learn to Understand and Express Empathy and Emotions* (2004) by Teresa A. Cardon. Shawnee Mission, KS: Autism Asperger Publishing Company; www.asperger.net. Copied with permission.

EMOTION: CONTENT

DEFINING

Dictionary Definition: _____

_____

_____

My Definition: _____

_____

_____

PERSPECTIVE TAKING

I have felt _____ when: _____

_____

_____

I noticed someone else was _____ when: _____

_____

_____

PROBLEM SOLVING

When I feel _____ I can:

1. _____

2. _____

3. _____

4. _____

A12

EmoTioN: HAPPY

DEFiNiNG

Dictionary Definition: _____

_____

_____

My Definition: _____

_____

_____

PERsPECTiVE TAKiNG

I have felt _____ when: _____

_____

_____

I noticed someone else was _____ when: _____

_____

_____

PRobLEm SoLViNG

When I feel _____ I can:

1. _____

2. _____

3. _____

4. _____

A13

Emotion: Proud

Defining

Dictionary Definition: _____

_____

_____

My Definition: _____

_____

_____

Perspective Taking

I have felt _____ when: _____

_____

_____

I noticed someone else was _____ when: _____

_____

_____

Problem Solving

When I feel _____ I can:

1. _____

2. _____

3. _____

4. _____

A14

From: *Let's Talk Emotions: Helping Children with Social Cognitive Disorders, Including AS, HFA, and NVLD, Learn to Understand and Express Empathy and Emotions* (2004) by Teresa A. Cardon. Shawnee Mission, KS: Autism Asperger Publishing Company; www.asperger.net. Copied with permission.

EMOTION: SURPRISED

DEFINING

Dictionary Definition: _____

_____

_____

My Definition: _____

_____

_____

PERSPECTIVE TAKING

I have felt _____ when: _____

_____

_____

I noticed someone else was _____ when: _____

_____

_____

PROBLEM SOLVING

When I feel _____ I can:

1. _____

2. _____

3. _____

4. _____

A15

EmoTioN: ExciTEd

DEFiNiNG

Dictionary Definition: _____

_____

_____

My Definition: _____

_____

_____

PERsPECTivE TAKiNG

I have felt _____ when: _____

_____

_____

I noticed someone else was _____ when: _____

_____

_____

PRoblEm SolviNG

When I feel _____ I can:

1. _____

2. _____

3. _____

4. _____

A16

From: Let's Talk Emotions: Helping Children with Social Cognitive Disorders, Including AS, HFA, and NVLD, Learn to Understand and Express Empathy and Emotions (2004) by Teresa A. Cardon. Shawnee Mission, KS: Autism Asperger Publishing Company; www.asperger.net. Copied with permission.

EMOTION: ELATED

DEFINING

Dictionary Definition: _____

_____

_____

My Definition: _____

_____

_____

PERSPECTIVE TAKING

I have felt _____ when: _____

_____

_____

I noticed someone else was _____ when: _____

_____

_____

PROBLEM SOLVING

When I feel _____ I can:

1. _____

2. _____

3. _____

4. _____

A17

EMOTION: _____

DEFINING

Dictionary Definition: _____
_____
_____

My Definition: _____
_____
_____

PERSPECTIVE TAKING

I have felt _____ when: _____
_____
_____

I noticed someone else was _____ when: _____
_____
_____

PROBLEM SOLVING

When I feel _____ I can:

1. _____

2. _____

3. _____

4. _____

A18

EMOTION: _____

DEFINING

Dictionary Definition: _____

_____

_____

My Definition: _____

_____

_____

PERSPECTIVE TAKING

I have felt _____ when: _____

_____

_____

I noticed someone else was _____ when: _____

_____

_____

PROBLEM SOLVING

When I feel _____ I can:

1. _____

2. _____

3. _____

4. _____

MY EMOTIONS JOURNAL
(Social Story)

I have a journal that I can use to express how I am feeling. When I am feeling upset about something, I can try writing down the experience in my journal. I may also want to write in my journal when something exciting or great happens to me. I may not remember all of the words that I want to use, but I can do my best to describe how I feel.

My journal is my own private book that I can choose to share when I am ready. Sharing my book may help someone else understand how I am feeling. When people understand how I am feeling, they may be able to help me.

I will feel better when I can write down my experiences in my emotions journal. Writing things down will help me work through my troubles. My family and friends will also be glad that they understand more about what I am feeling.

Note: This Social Story may be used in combination with the Emotions Journal activity (p. 19).

A20

From: *Let's Talk Emotions: Helping Children with Social Cognitive Disorders, Including AS, HFA, and NVLD, Learn to Understand and Express Empathy and Emotions* (2004) by Teresa A. Cardon. Shawnee Mission, KS: Autism Asperger Publishing Company; www.asperger.net. Copied with permission.

PicTuRe JouRNAl WoRKshEET

I FEEL **LIVID** whEN:

_____

_____

_____

_____

_____

_____

_____

A21

PicTuRE JouRNAL WoRKshEET

I FEEL ANGRY wHEN:

_____

_____

_____

_____

_____

_____

_____

A22

PICTURE JOURNAL WORKSHEET

I FEEL FRUSTRATED WHEN:

_____

_____

_____

_____

_____

_____

_____

A23

PicTuRe JouRNaL WoRKshEET

I FEEL SAD wHEN:

_____

_____

_____

_____

_____

_____

_____

PicTuRe JouRNAL WORKshEET

I FEEL **UPSET** wHEN:

_____

_____

_____

_____

_____

_____

_____

A25

PICTURE JOURNAL WORKSHEET

I FEEL CONTENT WHEN:

_____

_____

_____

_____

_____

_____

_____

A26

From: _Let's Talk Emotions: Helping Children with Social Cognitive Disorders, Including AS, HFA, and NVLD, Learn to Understand and Express Empathy and Emotions_ (2004) by Teresa A. Cardon. Shawnee Mission, KS: Autism Asperger Publishing Company; www.asperger.net. Copied with permission.

PICTURE JOURNAL WORKSHEET

I FEEL HAPPY WHEN:

_____

_____

_____

_____

_____

_____

_____

A27

PicTuRE JouRNAL WoRKshEET

I FEEL PROUD whEN:

_____

_____

_____

_____

_____

_____

_____

PICTURE JOURNAL WORKSHEET

I FEEL **SURPRISED** WHEN:

_____

_____

_____

_____

_____

_____

_____

A29

PICTURE JOURNAL WORKSHEET

I FEEL **EXCITED** WHEN:

_____

_____

_____

_____

_____

_____

_____

A30

PICTURE JOURNAL WORKSHEET

I FEEL ELATED WHEN:

_____

_____

_____

_____

_____

_____

_____

A31

PicTuRE JouRNAL WORKshEET

I FEEL _____ **WhEN:**

_____

_____

_____

_____

_____

_____

_____

A32

EмoTioNs DicTioNARY woRKsHEET

FaCiAL ExPREssioNs

Dictionary Definition: _____

_____

_____

My Definition: _____

_____

_____

ToNE

Dictionary Definition: _____

_____

_____

My Definition: _____

_____

_____

BodY LANguAgE

Dictionary Definition: _____

_____

_____

My Definition: _____

_____

_____

VoicE INfLEcTioN

Dictionary Definition: _____

_____

_____

My Definition: _____

_____

_____

A33

STORY ORGANIZER WORKSHEET

HIGH POINT

| RISING ACTION | | FALLING ACTION |

EVENT

RESOLUTION

1. What is the initial event? _____

_____

_____

2. What happens during the rising action of the event? _____

_____

_____

3. What emotion is present at the high point? _____

_____

_____

4. What happens during the falling action of the event? _____

_____

_____

5. What is a possible resolution of the event? _____

_____

_____

A34

From: *Let's Talk Emotions: Helping Children with Social Cognitive Disorders, Including AS, HFA, and NVLD, Learn to Understand and Express Empathy and Emotions* (2004) by Teresa A. Cardon. Shawnee Mission, KS: Autism Asperger Publishing Company; www.asperger.net. Copied with permission.

EMOTIONS DETECTIVE WORKSHEET

This week, be on the look-out for _____ .

Clues to look for are   _____

_____

_____

I FOUND A CLUE:

	Monday	Tuesday	Wednesday	Thursday	Friday	Saturday	Sunday
Morning							
Afternoon							
Evening							

Congratulations, detective!!! You are great at finding clues!!

A35

WHEEL OF EMOTIONS WORKSHEET

You feel HAPPY!

You and your friend
both had fun!

You share a toy
with your friend.

Your friend enjoys playing
with you and want to come again!

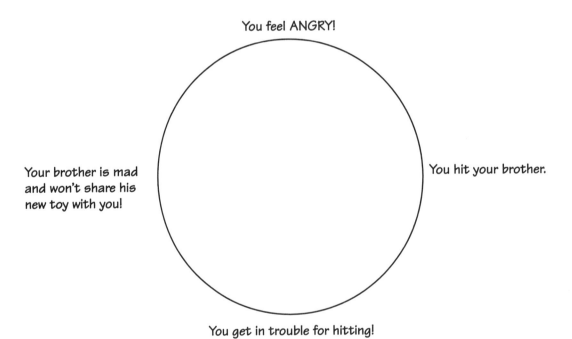

You feel ANGRY!

Your brother is mad
and won't share his
new toy with you!

You hit your brother.

You get in trouble for hitting!

A36

From: *Let's Talk Emotions: Helping Children with Social Cognitive Disorders, Including AS, HFA, and NVLD, Learn to Understand and Express Empathy and Emotions*
(2004) by Teresa A. Cardon. Shawnee Mission, KS: Autism Asperger Publishing Company; www.asperger.net. Copied with permission.

EMOTIONS ROLE-PLAYS AND SCENARIOS

1. You lose $5.00

2. You have to go to the dentist

3. Your pet frog died

4. You get an "A" in your math class

5. You find $10.00

6. It rains on "Fun in the Sun" day at school

7. You get a new video game

8. You are going to the zoo

9. You forgot to wear a helmet

10. You have to get a haircut

11. You get in a fight with your brother

12. You are sick and have to miss school

13. You had a bad dream

14. You get to pick out one special thing from the store

15. You get a new toy

16. Your dog is sick

17. Someone ruined your art project

18. You have to get a shot

19. You lose a tooth

20. You get to go ice skating

21. You get to go see a movie

A37

22. You rescue a cat from a tree

23. You miss the bus

24. Your pants rip

25. You are locked out of the house

26. You get to go to a friend's house

27. You have a game today

28. Your mom cooked your favorite dinner

29. Your new shirt got dirty

30. You are not finished with your homework

31. You lost the game

32. You won the game

33. You get to call your grandma

34. You get to go to the beach

35. You got sand in your shoes

36. Your mom is sick

37. You get to go to an amusement park

38. You have to go to bed

39. You broke you dad's watch

40. Your sister hits you

41. You forgot your jacket and it is cold outside

42. Your best friend is mad at you

43. Your friend gave you a present

44. You help set the table

A38

EMOTIONS

BINGO

B	I	N	G	O
Angry	Elated	Upset	Shy	Mischievous
Happy	Surprised	Excited	Confuse	Embarrassed
Silly	Proud	FREE	Tired	Grateful
Somber	Frustrated	Scared	Nervous	Betrayed
Livid	Content	Sad	Pleased	Bored

A39

From: *Let's Talk Emotions: Helping Children with Social Cognitive Disorders, Including AS, HFA, and NVLD, Learn to Understand and Express Empathy and Emotions*
(2004) by Teresa A. Cardon. Shawnee Mission, KS: Autism Asperger Publishing Company; www.asperger.net. Copied with permission.

EMOTIONS

B I N G O

Surprised	Elated	Happy	Bored	Livid
Upset	Angry	Excited	Confused	Embarrassed
Silly	Somber	FREE	Tired	Grateful
Proud	Frustrated	Sad	Nervous	Betrayed
Mischievous	Content	Scared	Pleased	Shy

A40

EMOTIONS

B I N G O

Livid	Frustrated	Excited	Pleased	Confused
Happy	Silly	Upset	Nervous	Embarrassed
Surprised	Proud	FREE	Tired	Betrayed
Somber	Elated	Scared	Mischievous	Bored
Angry	Sad	Content	Shy	Grateful

A41

EMOTIONS

B I N G O

Angry	Happy	Upset	Betrayed	Confused
Shy	Surprised	Scared	Pleased	Embarrassed
Silly	Proud	FREE	Tired	Grateful
Elated	Somber	Frustrated	Nervous	Mischievous
Livid	Content	Sad	Excited	Bored

A42

From: *Let's Talk Emotions: Helping Children with Social Cognitive Disorders, Including AS, HFA, and NVLD, Learn to Understand and Express Empathy and Emotions* (2004) by Teresa A. Cardon. Shawnee Mission, KS: Autism Asperger Publishing Company; www.asperger.net. Copied with permission.

EMOTIONS

B I N G O

Elated	Livid	Upset	Bored	Mischievous
Happy	Scared	Surprised	Confused	Embarrassed
Shy	Silly	FREE	Tired	Sad
Somber	Frustrated	Angry	Excited	Betrayed
Proud	Content	Nervous	Pleased	Grateful

A43

EMOTION

START	
EMOTION	
EMOTION	
EMOTION	EMOTION

EMOTION	
EMOTION	

A44

LAND

FINISH

EMOTION

EMOTION

EMOTION

EMOTION

EMOTION

EMOTION

EMOTION

A45

EMOTION LAND CARDS

You found five dollars outside a store. How do you feel? What do you do?	You ask a friend to come over and play. She can't make it today! How do you feel? What do you do?
Your brother took away your favorite toy. How do you feel? What do you do?	Your teacher thanks you for behaving so nicely in class. How do you feel? What do you do?
Your mom notices you cleaned your room without being asked. How do you feel? What do you do?	Your teacher asks for your homework. You left it at home. How do you feel? What do you do?
You got a grade on a test that you feel is unfair. How do you feel? What do you do?	You want to go to a movie, but your parents say the movie is not appropriate for kids your age. How do you feel? What do you do?

A46

EMOTION LAND CARDS

You are supposed to go to an assembly and you just don't feel like it. How do you feel? What do you do?	Your new video game isn't working. How do you feel? What do you do?
You got the highest grade in class on a math test! How do you feel? What do you do?	You get to go to the zoo today as long as it doesn't rain – uh-oh, it just started raining! How do you feel? What do you do?
You have to go to the dentist to have a cavity filled. How do you feel? What do you do?	You fell off your bike and scraped your knee! How do you feel? What do you do?
You got an "A" on a math test and your friend only got a "C." How do you feel? What do you do?	You are going to get a haircut this afternoon. How do you feel? What do you do?

A47

EMOTION LAND CARDS

You get in a fight with your brother/sister and have to go to your room! How do you feel? What do you do?	Your dog is sick and doesn't want to play with you. How do you feel? What do you do?
You wake up in the middle of the night because you had a bad dream! How do you feel? What do you do?	Someone ruined your art project that was hanging on the wall at school. How do you feel? What do you do?
There is a big party at school today. Everything will be different! How do you feel? What do you do?	Your teacher accidentally bumps your desk as she walks by. How do you feel? What do you do?
Your mom let you pick out one special thing at the store! How do you feel? What do you do?	Your mom just told you that you are going to the doctor to get a shot. How do you feel? What do you do?

A48

EMOTION LAND CARDS

You are sitting in class and you suddenly push your tooth out with your tongue. How do you feel? What do you do?	You are running late and you miss the school bus. How do you feel? What do you do?
Your pet frog isn't in the cage when you get home from school. How do you feel? What do you do?	Your favorite pants have a hole in them, and your mom wants to throw them away. How do you feel? What do you do?
You get to see a movie you have been wanting to see! How do you feel? What do you do?	You did not get to play in your soccer game yesterday. How do you feel? What do you do?
You help your neighbor bring in the trash cans. How do you feel? What do you do?	Your mom cooked your favorite meal for dinner. How do you feel? What do you do?

A49

EMOTION LAND CARDS

The shirt you wanted to wear to school today isn't clean. How do you feel? What do you do?	You get to invite a friend to go to the beach. How do you feel? What do you do?
Mom says it is time for bed and you are not finished with your homework. How do you feel? What do you do?	Your friends all have these cool new tennis shoes and yours are old. How do you feel? What do you do?
You were playing a video game and you couldn't get to the next level. How do you feel? What do you do?	Your mom isn't feeling well and you want to go to the store. How do you feel? What do you do?
Your grandma calls on the phone to say "hello." How do you feel? What do you do?	Someone took your pencil and you think you know who did it! How do you feel? What do you do?

A50

EMOTION LAND CARDS

You are going bowling for a birthday party. How do you feel? What do you do?	Your friend is mad at you and you don't know why. How do you feel? What do you do?
It is time to go to bed and your favorite show isn't over yet. How do you feel? What do you do?	You helped set the table for dinner. How do you feel? What do you do?
Your sister/brother went into your room without your permission. How do you feel? What do you do?	You accidentally broke your dad's new shovel. How do you feel? What do you do?
You left your jacket on the bus and you are cold. How do you feel? What do you do?	Lots of people are coming over for a big dinner party at your house. How do you feel? What do you do?

A51

From: *Let's Talk Emotions: Helping Children with Social Cognitive Disorders, Including AS, HFA, and NVLD, Learn to Understand and Express Empathy and Emotions* (2004) by Teresa A. Cardon. Shawnee Mission, KS: Autism Asperger Publishing Company; www.asperger.net. Copied with permission.

FACE

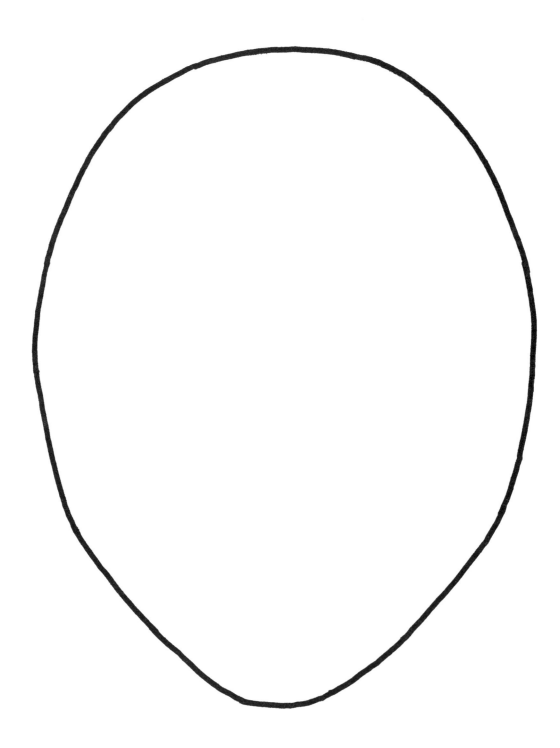

A52

EYEBROWS

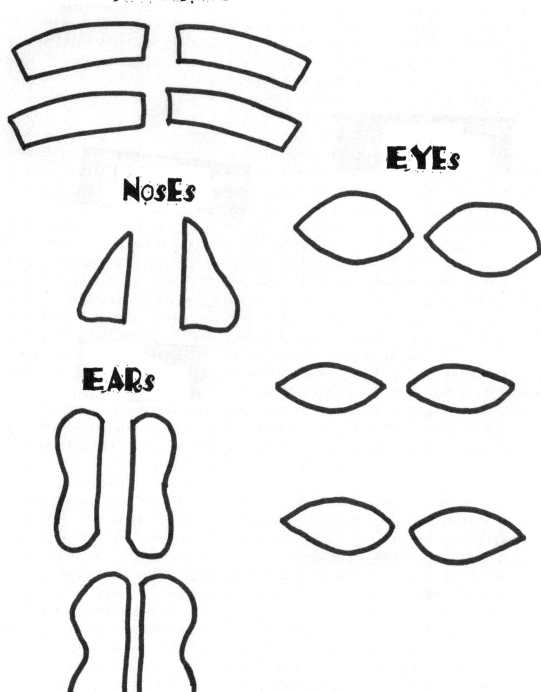

EYES

NOSES

EARS

A53

MouThs

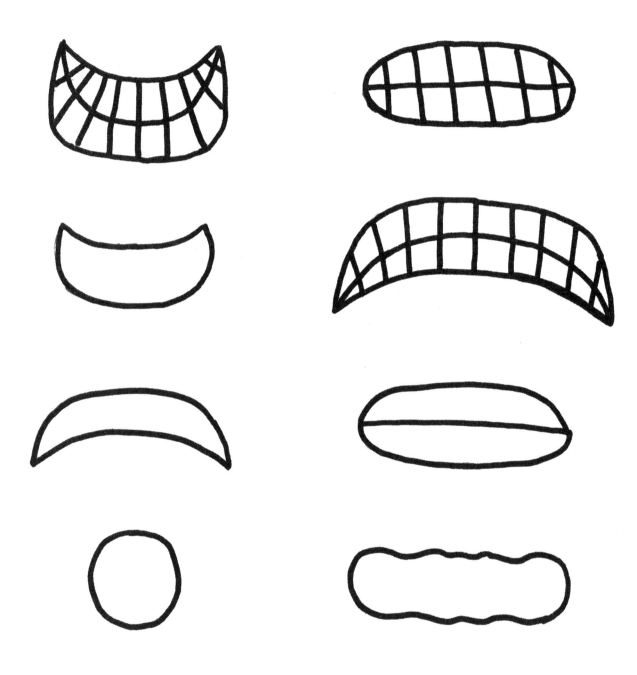

A54

CONTENT

A55

LIVID

A56

ANGRY

A57

SCARED

A58

SAD

A59

PROUD

A60

FRusTRATEd

A61

SuRPRisEd

A62

HAPPY

A63

EXCITED

A64

EMbARRAssEd

A65

More Favorable Reviews ...

"This book is a 'must have' for SLPs who work with children with social cognitive deficits. It is a wonderful tool that provides practical goals targeting empathy and emotions that are reinforced through easy-to-understand activities that can be used by SLPs and teachers as well as parents and other professionals."

— Amy Graham, MA, CCC-SLP
Speech-Language Pathologist
Summit Speech Pathology Services, Inc.

"This book is a great resource for helping children develop an emotion vocabulary. It provides wonderful goal ideas and activities to target these goals for a range of ages. Let's Talk Emotions would be a valuable part of any therapy library."

— Laura Richard
Speech-Language Pathologist

"The ability to identify and express intense and subtle emotions despite language and cultural barriers indicates the importance of nonverbal social skills, yet this area is often overlooked. Let's Talk Emotions is the first social training program I have found that provides practical and functional therapy activities to help my students understand and use appropriate emotional cues."

— Jordan Clark, M.S., CCC-SLP
Arizona Speech Works, LLC
Director of Camp Chit Chat